preteen Bible study series

Why God Made Me

Loveland, Colorado

Group's R.E.A.L. Guarantee to you:

This Group resource incorporates our R.E.A.L. approach to ministry—one that encourages long-term retention and life transformation. It's ministry that's:

Relational
Because learner-to-learner interaction enhances learning and builds Christian friendships.

Experiential
Because what learners experience through discussion and action sticks with them up to 9 times longer than what they simply hear or read.

Applicable
Because the aim of Christian education is to equip learners to be both hearers and doers of God's Word.

Learner-based
Because learners understand and retain more when the learning process takes into consideration how they learn best.

preteen Bible study series

Why God Made Me

Copyright © 2003 Group Publishing, Inc.

Visit our Web site: **www.grouppublishing.com**

Credits
Authors: Nancy S. Going, Cindy S. Hansen, and Norman D. Stolpe
Editor: Jim Hawley
Creative Development Editor: Karl Leuthauser
Chief Creative Officer: Joani Schultz
Copy Editor: Betty Taylor
Art Director: Kari K. Monson
Cover Art Director/Designer: Jeff A. Storm
Cover Photographer: Getty Images
Print Production Artist: Tracy K. Hindman
Illustrator: Shawn Banner
Production Manager: DeAnne Lear

Unless otherwise noted, Scripture taken from the HOLY BIBLE, NEW INTERNATIONAL VERSION®. Copyright © 1973, 1978, 1984 by International Bible Society. Used by permission of Zondervan Publishing House. All rights reserved.

ISBN 0-7644-2483-1
10 9 8 7 6 5 4 3 2 1   12 11 10 09 08 07 06 05 04 03

Printed in the United States of America.

Contents

Introduction:
Why God Made Me

Preteens are discovering a new world of possibilities. Many are entering middle school, where they are being stretched to learn new things and apply themselves in new ways. And they can be stretched in spiritual ways as well. Preteens are able to wrestle with basic questions such as "Why did God make me?" and "What should I do with my life?"

Why God Made Me will allow students to explore these questions. In the first study, they'll explore the creation of humankind. They will discover what it means to be made in God's image.

Next, preteens will explore what it means to care for others. They will look at the difference between genuine caring and simply pleasing someone to gain approval.

In the third study, your students will discover how God has given each of them wonder and unique abilities and gifts. They'll explore how to recognize and affirm the gifts God has given them.

God made people to glorify him in their everyday lives. But everyone, including preteens, falls short of this ideal. The last study will help preteens see how God's grace works in their lives when they fail. They'll see how God's forgiveness is a free gift, and they'll also be challenged to look beyond their failures, as they live victoriously in Jesus.

> Preteens are able to wrestle with basic questions such as "Why did God make me?" and "What should I do with my life?"

The Faith 4 Life: Preteen Bible Study Series helps preteens take a Bible-based approach to faith and life issues. Each book in the series contains these important elements:

- **Life application of Bible truth**—Faith 4 Life studies help preteens understand what the Bible says and then apply that truth to their lives.

- **A relevant topic**—Each Faith 4 Life book focuses on one main topic, with four studies to give your students a thorough understanding of how the Bible relates to that topic.

- **One point**—Each study makes one point, centering on that one theme to make sure students really understand the important truth it conveys. This point is stated upfront and throughout the study.

- **Simplicity**—The studies are easy to use. Each contains a "Before the Study" box that outlines any advance preparation required. Each study also contains a "Study at a Glance" chart so you can quickly and easily see what supplies you'll need and what each study will involve.

- **Action and interaction**—Each study relies on experiential learning to help students learn what God's Word has to say. Preteens discuss and debrief their experiences in large groups, small groups, and individual reflection.

- **Reproducible handouts**—Faith 4 Life books include reproducible handouts for students. No need for student books!

- **Flexible options**—Faith 4 Life preteen studies have two opening and two closing activities. You can choose the options that work best for your students, time frame, or supply needs.

- **Follow-up ideas**—At the end of each book, you'll find a section called "Changed 4 Life." This provides ideas for following up with your students to make sure the Bible truths stick with them.

Use Faith 4 Life studies to show your preteens how the Bible is relevant to their lives. Help them see that God can invade every area of their lives and change them in ways they can only imagine. Encourage your students to go deeper into faith—faith that will sustain them for life! Faith 4 Life, forever!

Made in God's Image

The Point: ➤ Humans are created in God's image to glorify him.

Body image is an important concern for preteens. They are maturing at different rates, and they experience the pressure to compare how they look with how others look—especially when they think others look better. When preteens hear that they are a wonderful creation of God and are made in his image, they may feel disappointed in how they look and wonder how God could make them that way.

Use this study to help preteens understand the differences between body image and God's image, and to accept themselves as God has created them.

Scripture Source

Genesis 1:26-31; 2:15-23

This passage gives the account of humankind's creation. God states he created humans in his image and gave them dominion over the animals and charged them with caring for nature.

Isaiah 52:13–53:3

Isaiah describes the suffering servant, believed to be a messianic prophecy describing Christ. The prophecy details the humble appearance of the servant and his being horribly disfigured.

2 Corinthians 4:16-18

Paul describes how the earthly body is decaying, but our spiritual lives are being renewed in preparation for an eternity with God.

2 Corinthians 12:7-10

Paul described his "thorn in the flesh." Whether it was a physical aliment or something else, Paul prayed for healing, but God gave him the assurance that his grace was enough for this situation.

Ephesians 4:13

Paul writes that the goal of Christian growth is to be conformed to Jesus' image.

The Study at a Glance

Section	Minutes	What Students Will Do	Supplies
Warm-Up Option 1	up to 10	**My Sculpture**—Create sculptures that show their inner qualities.	Soft modeling compound or clay
Warm-Up Option 2	up to 10	**Image Pictures**—Guess words from humankind's creation as volunteers draw them.	Newsprint, markers, paper
Bible Connection	up to 15	**Image Isn't Looks**—Explore physical limitations of Isaiah's servant described in Isaiah 52–53 and of Paul described in 2 Corinthians.	Bibles, paper, pens, newsprint, marker
	up to 10	**In God's Image**—Explore humankind's creation in Genesis 1–2 and list ways that people are similar to and different from God.	Bibles, "Same and Different" handouts (p. 13), pens
Life Application	up to 15	**Living God's Image**—Read Ephesians 4:13 and create skits about living as Christ did.	Bible
Wrap-Up Option 1	up to 5	**Living Image Prayer**—As a closing prayer, list ways they will live out showing God's image.	
Wrap-Up Option 2	up to 10	**Creation Praises**—Write new words for a familiar hymn or song, praising God for humankind's creation.	Paper, pens, hymnals or song books

Before the Study

Set out Bibles, soft modeling compound or clay, newsprint, markers, paper, pens, and hymnals or song books. Also make a photocopy of the "Same and Different" handout (p. 13) for each preteen.

The Study

Warm-Up Option 1

My Sculpture *(up to 10 minutes)*

Have preteens form groups of up to five, and have groups brainstorm human character traits. Provide paper and pens to groups, and have a recorder list group responses. Circulate among groups and assist them as needed. Allow a few minutes for groups to complete a list of character traits. Then give each preteen a lump of soft modeling compound or clay. **Say: Out of this clay, you're each going to create a symbol for a character trait that best describes you. For example, if you're a patient person, you might form the clay into a clock without hands to**

represent patience. If you're a loving person, you might form a heart to represent love. Choose a quality you know describes you well.

After about three minutes or when kids have completed their sculptures, have them each briefly explain their sculptures.

Ask:

• **How did you feel as you created something out of clay?**

• **Was it easy to create something that represented a positive quality you have? Why or why not?**

Say: All of us have positive qualities because God made us in his image. We're beginning a series that looks at a variety of reasons why God made us. Today's topic begins with the beginning—discovering that ➤humans are created in God's image to glorify him. Let's get started.

◀ The Point

Warm-Up Option 2

Image Pictures *(up to 10 minutes)*

Form groups of up to four. Have each group find a place in the room away from the other groups. Give each group newsprint and markers. Have each group choose one person to be the artist, and have the artist from each group come up to you. Show each artist the first word on the "Game Words" list (while covering the rest of the words with a sheet of paper). Explain to artists that they are to go back to their groups and draw pictures depicting the word you've just showed them. Tell the artists not to talk or write letters of the word. **Say: Your group's artist has been shown a word that he or she must try to draw for your group, without talking or drawing the letters of the word. When someone in your group has correctly guessed the word, he or she will become the new artist, come up to get the next word, and follow the same rules. When your group has discovered all five words, decide in your group what you think the words mean.**

Begin the game. Continue to play until kids have uncovered all five words from your list.

Game Words

Life

Created

Good

Image

Breath

FYI

You may need to ask artists how many words they have uncovered so you can keep track of each group's progress and don't reveal more than the correct word for each group.

Ask:

• Was it easy to create pictures representing the various words? Explain.

• What do you think the words have in common?

Say: You may have noticed a theme in the words you were trying to draw and guess. That theme connects to the new series we're beginning today that looks at a variety of reasons God made us. So let's start with the beginning—discovering that ➤humans are created in God's image to glorify him. Let's get started.

Bible Connection

Image Isn't Looks *(up to 15 minutes)*

Form groups of up to four. Provide Bibles, paper, and pens to each group. **Say: Before we look at reasons why God made us, let's spend some time exploring the idea of being made in God's image.**

Ask:

• **What do you think the phrase "made in God's image" means?**

• **Do you think the physical qualities of people are an important part of this definition? Explain.**

Say: Let's look at some physical descriptions of people in the Bible.

List the following Scripture passages on newsprint: Isaiah 52:13–53:3; 2 Corinthians 4:16-18; and 12:7-10.

Have groups find the Scriptures in their Bibles and discuss the physical descriptions of the people described in the passages. Allow volunteers from each group to report their findings. **Say: These verses include several physical limitations of the Apostle Paul and give Isaiah's description of someone many believe to be Jesus.**

Ask:

• **If God uses people who aren't physically perfect, what does that say about being created in God's image?**

Say: Our culture places a lot of emphasis on looks. Everyday we see pictures of people in popular media who we may wish we looked like. But the reality for most of us is we must live with the physical characteristics we were born with. Although our physical characteristics are a part of being made in God's image, there is more to it than that. Let's explore further.

In God's Image *(up to 10 minutes)*

Provide a Bible, a "Same and Different" handout (p. 13), and a pen to each pre-teen. Have students form new groups of up to four and work together to complete their handouts. Then have groups discuss the following questions in their groups.

Ask:

- **What did you discover about being created in God's image?**

- **What makes humans unique?**

- **How do you think knowing you're created in God's image affects the way you live each day as a Christian?**

Say: It's awesome to think about how ➤humans are created in God's image to glorify him. And because of this, God want's us to live up to his image in each of us. That may seem a tough challenge, but each of us has at least one quality that matches how God would want us to live. Let's explore this now.

Life Application

Living God's Image *(up to 15 minutes)*

Ask a volunteer to read aloud Ephesians 4:13 to the class. **Say: In this passage Paul talks about becoming like Christ, which is how we can live up to God's image.**

Have students form groups of up to five people. Ask groups to create short skits that show how they are becoming like Christ. For example, they may show someone resisting pressure to cheat on a test or someone sharing faith with friends at school.

Allow a few minutes for kids to create their skits, and then have groups perform their skits for the class. Then

ask:

- **What can we do in our lives to better reflect the image of God in us?**

Allow a few volunteers each to share one thing they'll do to better reflect God's image. **Say: Let's close by showing our thanks for being created in God's image.**

Wrap-Up Option 1

Living Image Prayer *(up to 5 minutes)*

We've been discovering that ➤humans are created in God's image to glorify him. I want each of you to think of one specific way in which you will show God's image this week.

◄ *The Point*

◄ *The Point*

Have students form a circle, and allow each student to say his or her desire as a closing prayer. Begin and end the prayer, including in the prayer your expression of showing God's image in your life.

Wrap-Up Option 2

Creation Praises *(up to 10 minutes)*

Have kids choose a familiar hymn or song they enjoy singing. Then form groups of up to four, and have each group write a new verse for the song that describes the wonder of God's human creation. Have hymnals or song books available so kids can match words to the song.

Allow a few minutes for groups to write their verses. Then form a circle, and have kids each say one thing they like about being created in God's image. Close by having each group sing its verse of the song.

Extra-Time Tips

Portrait of God—Give preteens paper and pens, and have them draw "portraits" of God. Encourage kids to draw pictures that represent the qualities God has shared with us by making us in his image. For example, kids might draw images representing compassion, love, and mercy.

Creation Celebration—Form groups of up to four. Allow a few minutes for groups to create a four-line poem or cheer about God's creation. Then have groups recite their poems or do their cheers, one after the other, as a celebration of God's creation.

Same and Different

What does it mean to be created in God's image? Read about the creation of people in Genesis 1:26-31 and 2:15-23, and then answer the questions below based on what you discover about God and yourself.

How do people differ from animals?

What does it mean to have dominion over the animals and plants?

In what ways are people similar to God?

How are people different from God?

What does it mean to be created in God's image?

Being a Caring Person

The Point: ➤ God wants us to care for others, not merely please them.

Preteens often feel bad when they don't live up to others' expectations. And sometimes, others' expectations may shape how preteens act. Preteens may begin to please others to feel accepted.

Use this study to help preteens understand the difference between caring about others and simply pleasing them to gain acceptance.

Scripture Source

Matthew 16:13-20

Jesus asked Peter what others were saying about him. Peter gave Jesus various responses before telling him his belief that Jesus was the Christ. Throughout his ministry, Jesus met people who felt he didn't live up to their expectations of him. But he did live up to God's expectations.

Luke 7:36-50

While Jesus was dining with the Pharisees, a woman who had "lived a sinful life" came to Jesus, poured perfume on him, and washed his feet with her tears. In response to the Pharisees' disapproval, Jesus told a simple parable and directed it at the response of the Pharisee Simon. The parable is about two people—one with a large debt and the other with a small debt—forgiven by the same creditor, and Jesus asked which person would be more grateful. Jesus applied the parable to the woman, who was forgiven the large debt. This was in contrast to Simon the Pharisee having the lesser debt.

Acts 6:8-14

Some Jewish leaders opposed Stephen's ministry. While Stephen spoke the words God's Spirit gave him, some Jewish leaders stirred up others to accuse Stephen and to discredit his ministry.

Galatians 1:10-12

Paul defended his ministry to the Galatian Christians. Paul insisted he wasn't trying to win the approval of the people, but that the gospel he preached to them is the true gospel revealed to him by Jesus.

James 2:1-4

James admonishes Christians to avoid favoritism. He gives the example of a wealthy person and a poor person being treated differently in church. He condemns the practice of giving the wealthy preferred treatment.

1 Peter 3:13-16

Peter encourages Christians to be respectful of unbelievers. He urges believers to be ready to give answers to questions about their faith, but to do it in a gentle way.

The Study at a Glance

Section	Minutes	What Students Will Do	Supplies
Warm-Up Option 1	up to 10	**Picture Me**—Write positive comments about one another's pictures.	Instant-print camera with film, tape, paper, pens
Warm-Up Option 2	up to 10	**Your Favorite Things**—Guess one another's favorite things.	
Bible Connection	up to 15	**Caring Expectations**—Mime actions illustrating how others see them and explore caring actions in various Scriptures.	Bibles, paper, pens
	up to 15	**Caring or Pleasing?**—Explore examples of how Jesus dealt with the pressure to please others.	Bibles, "Jesus and Others" handouts (p. 22), pens
Life Application	up to 10	**My Motivation**—Evaluate what they do for others and for themselves.	"Why I Do What I Do" handouts (p. 23), pens
Wrap-Up Option 1	up to 5	**From the Heart**—Write ways they can be true to their hearts while caring about others.	Paper, markers
Wrap-Up Option 2	up to 5	**Help Me Do It for You, God**—Reflect on their motivation for what they do.	

Before the Study

Set out Bibles, paper, pens, tape, and markers. If you choose Warm-Up Option 1, you'll need an instant-print camera with enough film to take a picture of each preteen. Also make photocopies of the "Jesus and Others" handout (p. 22) and the "Why I Do What I Do" handout (p. 23) for each preteen.

The Study

Warm-Up Option 1

Picture Me *(up to 10 minutes)*

Take an instant-print picture of each student. Mix up the pictures, and pass them out. Have each student tape the picture he or she receives to a piece of paper. Then have preteens write up to five words or phrases on the paper to describe that person in a positive way. For example, someone might write, "likes music" or "gets good grades." Remind kids to be sincere. If someone doesn't know the person in the picture, encourage that person to guess about him or her on the basis of the picture. **Say: People assume things about you by how you look or act. At times, what they expect and who you really are may be very different.**

Have kids give the pictures back to their original owners. Then have each preteen explain how much of what was written is true and how much is false. **Say: Often others' expectations shape how we act or what we say. Today we're going to study the difference between trying to meet others' expectations and learning to care about others.** ▶**God wants us to care for others, not merely please them. Let's discover how.**   ◀*The Point*

Warm-Up Option 2

Your Favorite Things *(up to 10 minutes)*

Form a circle, and have one preteen stand in the center of the circle. If you have a large class, form circles of six to eight kids each. Have students guess the following things about the person in the circle.

Ask:

- **What's this person's favorite color?**
- **What's this person's favorite free-time activity?**
- **What's this person's favorite class in school?**
- **What's this person's favorite food?**

After kids have guessed the answers for the person in the center of the circle, have the person tell how he or she would honestly answer the questions. Repeat the activity until all kids have had a turn in the center of the circle.

Say: How others perceive us can affect how we act. If someone expects us to be loud, it's probably easy to be loud. Sometimes we begin to focus on meeting others' expectations instead of caring for others. Today we'll look at how we can care for others—and still be ourselves. ➤God wants us to care for others, not merely please them. Let's discover how.

The Point ➤

Bible Connection

Caring Expectations *(up to 15 minutes)*

Form groups of up to four, and have each group form a circle. Have students stand facing inward. Then have them each mime an action or activity that fits the following categories:

• The image my friends have of me is…

• The image my parents have of me is…

• The image I have of myself is…

Encourage kids to use facial expressions and motions to illustrate the images. Then have kids discuss these questions in their groups.

Ask:

• **Was there a difference in your actions from one category to the next? Explain.**

• **How did you feel about acting differently for each category?**

• **Do others' expectations of how you should act affect how you act? Why or why not?**

Say: When we act according to others' expectations, it's often because we want to please them or be accepted. But when we seek to please others, it sometimes keeps us from being ourselves. Instead of striving to please others, we should learn to be ourselves and care for others. Let's look at some examples of this.

Assign one of the following Bible passages to each group: Acts 6:8-14; Galatians 1:10-12; James 2:1-4; and 1 Peter 3:13-16. Have each group choose the following roles: a reader to read the passages aloud, a recorder to record the group's findings, a reporter to share the group's responses with the class, and an encourager to keep the

FYI

Whenever groups discuss a list of questions, write the questions on newsprint, and tape the newsprint to the wall so groups can discuss the questions at their own pace.

group on track. **Say: In your groups, explore these Bible passages, and look for examples of how people were cared for in these situations or for principles you could apply toward caring for people.**

Allow groups about five minutes to work through the passages and record their findings. When groups are ready, have a reporter from each group share the group's discoveries.

Ask:

• **How did your examples help you see how to care for people?**

• **Did the care demonstrated in your situation please the people involved? Why or why not?**

Say: ➤ God wants us to care for others, not merely please them. Sometimes, as we've just seen, that may not be easy. Even Jesus faced this situation.

◀ The Point

Caring or Pleasing? *(up to 15 minutes)*

Say: Jesus dealt with the issue of how to please others. He also dealt with others' expectations.

Give each preteen a copy of the "Jesus and Others" handout (p. 22). Form new groups of up to four. Have each group read Matthew 16:13-20 and Luke 7:36-50. Have groups discuss the questions based on the passages.

Then have each group brainstorm two or three differences between pleasing someone and caring for someone. Have each group report these differences to the other groups.

Ask:

• **How did Jesus care for others?**

Say: Jesus knew his mission was different from what many people thought it should be. But he didn't change his ways to please others. Instead, he used who he was to care for others. Let's see how well we do this.

Life Application

My Motivation *(up to 10 minutes)*

Give each preteen a copy of the "Why I Do What I Do" handout (p. 23). Have students follow the instructions and complete their handouts. Explain that they won't have to share their answers.

Ask:

- **How does this handout give you a clearer idea of who you are?**

- **How do you feel about the items you've marked, "Because I want to"?**

- **How do you feel about the items you marked, "Because others expect me to"?**

- **Based on your answers, do you do things because of who you are or because of others' expectations? Why?**

Say: God wants us to be who we are and to develop as individuals. He wants us to care for others because we want to—not because we feel we have to.

Wrap-Up Option 1

From the Heart *(up to 5 minutes)*

Give each student a piece of paper and a marker. Have each preteen quickly tear the paper into the shape of a heart. Then have kids form a circle. **Say: When we do things because others expect us to, we may be untrue to ourselves. Instead, God wants us to do things from the heart.**

Have kids each write on their paper heart one way they can be true to who God made them as they care for others.

Close by having each preteen silently complete the following sentence as a prayer to God after you read it aloud: **Say: One way I can strive to be who God wants me to be is...**

Wrap-Up Option 2

Help Me Do It for You, God *(up to 5 minutes)*

Have preteens reflect on the responses they wrote on the "Why I Do What I Do" handout from the previous activity. Have them spread out and take a few minutes in silent reflection and prayer.

After a few minutes,

Say: Just as Jesus didn't compromise who he was to please others, we need to avoid compromising who we are. We need to show people we truly care about them.

Have students form a circle. Ask preteens to each think of one way they can care for someone this week. Then, as a closing prayer, ask God to help preteens live out their plans.

Masks—Have students describe "masks" people wear when they try to please others. Then have kids discuss how they feel when they put on masks or see people who put on masks.

Who God Wants—Form groups of up to four. Have groups each come up with a poem or a rap song that describes who God wants them to be.

Jesus and Others

Read Matthew 16:13-20 and Luke 7:36-50.

• Who did people think Jesus was?

• How do you feel when people describe you as being like someone else?

• Did Jesus change his actions to meet others' expectations? Why or why not?

• Did Jesus try to please others or care for them? Explain.

• How did Jesus care for people in these passages?

Why I Do What I Do

For each item, place a mark in the column that best describes why you do it.

	Because I want to	**Because others expect me to**	**Doesn't apply**
1. I try to get good grades.	❏	❏	❏
2. I try to be funny.	❏	❏	❏
3. I do things to make people happy.	❏	❏	❏
4. I help others.	❏	❏	❏
5. I follow the rules.	❏	❏	❏
6. I strive to be good at sports.	❏	❏	❏
7. I try to be popular.	❏	❏	❏
8. I do what my friends are doing.	❏	❏	❏
9. I like certain kinds of music.	❏	❏	❏
10. I make money.	❏	❏	❏
11. I help friends with homework.	❏	❏	❏
12. I read my Bible.	❏	❏	❏
13. I go to church.	❏	❏	❏
14. I spend time praying.	❏	❏	❏

God's Wonderful Gifts

The Point: ➤ God has given each of us unique gifts and abilities to serve him.

Sometimes it's easier for preteens to see others' strengths and abilities than it is to see their own. When they don't see their own abilities, they may feel inferior or rejected. But preteens can be encouraged as they learn to recognize their own unique qualities.

Use this study to help preteens discover and affirm their God-given gifts and abilities.

Scripture Source

John 6:32-36; 8:12-16; 10:14-17; and 11:20-27

Jesus describes himself with "I am" statements. In each of these short passages, Jesus reveals something about himself. He describes himself as the "bread of life," "the light of the world," "the good shepherd," and "the resurrection and the life." Each phrase sheds light on both the nature of Jesus and his mission on earth. Jesus knew who he was and how important it was to be connected with God's will.

Romans 12:4-8

Paul describes spiritual gifts. He explains how different gifts are given to different people, so that the body of Christ is served. The Holy Spirit empowers Christians with the various spiritual gifts to use in Christian service.

The Study at a Glance

Section	Minutes	What Students Will Do	Supplies
Warm-Up Option 1	up to 10	**Unique Pictures**—Identify their unique qualities in baby pictures.	Baby pictures, tape, paper, pens
Warm-Up Option 2	up to 10	**Creation Mural**—Create murals of things God created.	Magazines, tape, newsprint
Bible Connection	up to 20	**Unique People, Unique Gifts**—Interview their partners to discover their unique characteristics before exploring spiritual gifts in Romans 12.	Bibles, "Unique Interview" handouts (p. 31), pens
	up to 10	**I Am**—Explore Jesus' "I am" statements in John and discuss Jesus' uniqueness and how he used his abilities.	Bibles, newsprint, markers
Life Application	up to 10	**Serving God**—Role play situations in which they use their gifts and abilities to serve God.	
Wrap-Up Option 1	up to 10	**Unique Creation**—Create symbols to affirm each other as God's creation.	Paper, tape
Wrap-Up Option 2	up to 5	**Thanks for My Gifts**—Identify gifts and thank God for them.	

Before the Study

Set out Bibles, paper, pens, tape, nature and people magazines, newsprint, and markers. Also make a photocopy of the "Unique Interview" handout (p. 31) for each preteen. If you choose Warm-Up Option 1, contact preteens, and have them each bring in a baby picture from home, or collect pictures from parents before the study.

The Study

Warm-Up Option 1

Unique Pictures *(up to 10 minutes)*

You'll need the baby pictures you asked students to bring in earlier for this activity. Collect the baby pictures from students. Carefully tape the pictures to a wall. Under each picture, tape a piece of paper with a number on it. Have each student write on a blank piece of paper the numbers from the pictures. Then give them a few minutes to look over the pictures, silently guess who's who, and write their guesses next to the appropriate numbers on their papers. Tell kids not to help one another.

When everyone has finished, go through the pictures and have kids tell who they think is in each picture. After they've guessed correctly, ask what unique feature helped them make an accurate guess.

Ask:

• **What features made it easy to guess some of the pictures?**

Say: Just as each of the babies in these pictures has unique features, so each of us has unique abilities and gifts. But finding these gifts is sometimes as hard as identifying the right person in these baby pictures. Today we're going to explore how ➤God has given each of us unique gifts and abilities to serve him. ◀ *The Point*

Warm-Up Option 2

Creation Mural (up to 10 minutes)

Form groups large enough to allow preteens to gather around tables. Place pieces of newsprint on the tables. Distribute tape and magazines that have both nature and people pictures in them. Have kids silently tear out pictures and words representing God's creation and then tape them to the pieces of newsprint. After a few minutes, hang the murals and have students gather around them.

Ask:

• **Are there any major elements missing from this mural? Explain.**

• **Which picture best represents God's creation to you? Explain.**

• **Based on the pictures on the wall, does everyone enjoy the same parts of God's creation? Explain.**

Say: God created a varied and interesting world around us. And he also created a variety of people to inhabit the world. Today we're going to explore how ➤God has given each of us unique gifts and abilities to serve him. ◀ *The Point*

Bible Connection

Unique People, Unique Gifts (up to 20 minutes)

Have preteens form pairs. Give each student a copy of the "Unique Interview" handout (p. 31) and a pen. **Say: In your pair, take turns asking each other a question from the handout, and write your partner's response on your handout. Answer the first nine questions, but stop there. We'll cover the last question later.**

Allow students adequate time to complete the first nine questions of the interview with their partners. Then have partners discuss the following questions with each other.

Ask:

- **What response from your partner surprised you most? Why?**
- **How different were your partner's answers from yours?**
- **Was it easy or hard to identify a unique talent of yours? Explain.**

Say: We all are created unique and have different interests and abilities. Not only does God give you these abilities, he also gives us special gifts to serve him with. Let's look at those.

Provide Bibles to pairs, and have a volunteer in each pair read aloud Romans 12:4-8. **Say: Now take turns answering the last question on your handout. Think about the gifts in the Bible passage as you answer this question.**

After students have answered the last question,

ask:

- **What spiritual gift or gifts do you think God has given you?**

Allow a few volunteers to share responses. **Say: This activity has helped us**

The Point ▶

see how ▶God has given each of us unique gifts and abilities to serve him. It's important to identify your unique abilities and gifts. After you do, you can begin using those gifts. Next we'll take a look at how Jesus used his gifts.

I Am *(up to 10 minutes)*

Form groups of up to four. Assign each group one of the following Scriptures: John 6:32-36; 8:12-16; 10:14-17; and 11:20-27. Give each group Bibles, a sheet of newsprint, and markers. Have a reader in each group read the assigned passage, and then have group members discuss how they saw Jesus use his gifts. Then have each group draw a picture or symbol that shows who Jesus says he is or how he uses his abilities. Allow each group to select a reporter to present the drawing to the class. After all the groups have shared,

ask:

- **How did Jesus describe himself?**
- **How did he use his gifts and abilities to do God's will?**

Say: Jesus is the perfect example of serving God with his gifts. Whatever our gifts, God wants us to use them to his glory. Let's practice this idea now.

Serving God *(up to 10 minutes)*

Have preteens remain in their groups from the previous activity. Instruct each group to choose a gift or ability of one of the members, and create a short skit showing how the gift or ability is being used. For example, for the gift of encouraging, kids could show one person who is left out of a group, and then show another person coming over to invite that person to join his or her group.

Allow students a few minutes to prepare and present their skits. After skits have been presented,

ask:

• **How does it feel to know God has given you unique gifts and abilities?**

• **How do you think you can use your abilities and gifts to serve God?**

Say: ➤God has given each of us unique gifts and abilities. And it's exciting to think about how God will use us and our abilities to serve him!   ◀ *The Point*

Wrap-Up Option 1

Unique Creation *(up to 10 minutes)*

Have preteens form pairs. Provide paper and tape to each student. Have each partner tear, fold, tape, or otherwise form the paper into a unique, three-dimensional symbol that represents his or her partner's God-given ability. Then have kids present their creations to their partners and say at least one thing they appreciate about the partners' God-given abilities. Remind kids to be sincere because that's a great way to show God's love.

Form a circle, and have students hold up their creations. Go around the circle and have each student share what the creation represents about his or her partner. Encourage preteens to keep their paper creations as reminders of God's creation of them as unique individuals.

Wrap-Up Option 2

Thanks for My Gifts *(up to 5 minutes)*

Say: Think of one gift or ability you are most thankful for.

Have students form a circle. Tell students a gift you're thankful for, and then ask each preteen to say aloud his or her gift or ability. Then have each student share one way he or she could use his or her gift or ability to glorify God. Close in prayer, thanking God for the unique way he gifts each person.

Extra-Time Tips

Who Am I?—Have kids play the Who Am I? game. Have each preteen think of someone living or dead. Then have each student write three sentences that person might say that would describe him or her. Read the sentences aloud, and have kids guess who the sentences describe. Afterward, discuss how people become known for certain abilities or characteristics. Then have students write three sentences that describe themselves. Collect the sentences, and read them without revealing who wrote them. Have kids guess who wrote the sentences.

Ability Cards—Give each preteen an index card and a pen. Have each student sign the card and write on it one ability or talent he or she has that could be used to help someone in the class. For example, someone might write that he or she is good in math and could help tutor someone. Collect the cards. Then pass the cards around the room. Have students read the cards and silently decide how they might benefit from someone else's abilities.

Unique Interview

Interview your partner and record the information below:

1. My favorite subject in school is... ______________________________

____

2. The thing I like to do most with my free time is... ______________________

____

3. My favorite sport to watch or play is... ______________________

____

4. The most interesting place I've visited is... ______________________

____

5. What I think I want to do for a career is... ______________________

____

6. My favorite hobby is... ______________________

____

7. One of the best times of my life was when... ______________________

____

8. The thing I want most from my friends is... ______________________

____

9. One unique talent I have is... ______________________

____

10. One way I think I could use my talent for God is...______________________

____

Accepting God's Grace

The Point: ➤We can live for God because of Jesus' forgiveness.

Everybody falls short of living for God. Preteens are no exception. As they begin to understand the nature of sin in their lives, preteens may have a hard time accepting God's free grace. At the same time, they could use the excuse of receiving God's grace as justification for their sin.

Use this study to help preteens embrace God's grace when they sin and to strive to live for God more fully in their lives.

Scripture Source

Luke 15:11-32

Jesus tells the story of the prodigal (lost) son. A son demanded his inheritance from his father and squandered it on wild living. While broke, hungry, and desperate, the son returned home, hoping his father would make him a servant. But the father celebrated his son's return, throwing a huge banquet. The older son was resentful of the younger son's return. But the father explained to his older son how he had always been his son, and now the father had regained his lost son as well.

Luke 22:52-62

Jesus was interrogated while Peter denied knowing Jesus three times. Jesus had predicted that Peter would deny him, and Peter denied knowing Jesus to three different people. When the rooster crowed and Jesus looked at him, Peter realized his sin and broke down.

John 1:16-18

John introduced his Gospel by proclaiming how God's grace in Jesus supersedes the law of Moses. He also states Jesus' earthly ministry has made God known.

John 21:15-19

Jesus reinstated Peter when he appeared to his disciples. Just as Peter had denied Jesus three times, Jesus asked Peter three times whether he loved him. Peter replied he did, and then Jesus told Peter that Peter would care for God's people and would also face a difficult death in his old age.

Ephesians 2:8-9

Paul explains how grace saves us. In contrast with the idea that good works are a means to salvation, Paul explains that God gives salvation because of faith in Christ—and not humans' works.

Philippians 3:12-14

Paul encourages us to look to what lies ahead. Using the language of an athlete, Paul explained how he strove to win the prize of heaven, forgetting past failures.

Hebrews 4:14-16

Jesus' role as high priest is explained. Jesus took on the human role of the high priest as he was sacrificed on the cross. He knew the temptations of humankind, yet remained sinless. Because of his sacrifice, Christians can approach God with confidence.

1 John 2:1-2

John encourages Christians not to sin. He explains how Jesus speaks to God to forgive us when we do sin, forgiveness made possible by Jesus' sacrifice on the cross.

The Study at a Glance

Section	Minutes	What Students Will Do	Supplies
Warm-Up Option 1	up to 10	**Tricky Trivia**—Play a trivia game and discuss failing.	Trivia game cards
Warm-Up Option 2	up to 10	**Missing the Mark**—Attempt to toss a ball at a target and discuss the meaning of sin.	Roll of masking tape, newsprint, marker
Bible Connection	up to 10	**What Is Grace?**—Explore Scriptures about grace and write personal grace statements.	Bibles, "God's Grace for Me" handouts (p. 39), pens
	up to 20	**Forgiveness Stories**—Act out Bible stories from Luke 15 and 22 and John 21, and discuss forgiveness.	Bibles
Life Application	up to 10	**Forgiveness Thanks**—Reflect on Philippians 3:12-14 and write letters of thanks to God.	Bibles, "Forgiveness Letter" handouts (p. 40), pens
Wrap-Up Option 1	up to 10	**Forgiveness Banquet**—Have refreshments and celebrate God's forgiveness.	Snacks, drinks, CD player, praise CDs
Wrap-Up Option 2	up to 10	**Clean Slate**—See how their forgiven sins are like a clean sheet of paper.	Paper, marker

Before the Study

Set out Bibles, Trivia game cards, newsprint, markers, paper, pens, and tape. If you chose Wrap-Up Option 1, have available snacks, drinks, CD player, and praise or worship CDs. If you choose Warm-Up Option 2, see the instructions for preparing the target and ball at the bottom of this page. Also make a photocopy of the "God's Grace for Me" handout (p. 39) and of the "Forgiveness Letter" handout (p. 40) for each preteen.

The Study

Warm-Up Option 1

Tricky Trivia *(up to 10 minutes)*

Form two groups if your class has twelve students or fewer. Form four groups if your class has more than twenty students. Explain that you'll read five questions to each group. First read three easy questions to each group from a popular trivia game. Then read two very difficult questions to each group. Be sure at least one question for each group is too difficult for anyone to answer.

Ask:

- **How did you feel after you'd answered the first questions correctly?**
- **How did you feel when you failed to answer a question?**

Say: In this game, it wasn't that big a deal to fail to answer a question correctly. But in real life, our failures may be more serious. God has given us both his Word and his Holy Spirit to help us live for him. But when we fail to live for him in small or big ways, God's grace offers us forgiveness. Today's we're going to see how ➤We can live for God because of Jesus' forgiveness. Let's explore this more. ◄ *The Point*

Warm-Up Option 2

Missing the Mark *(up to 10 minutes)*

Make a masking tape ball before this activity. Wrap several feet of masking tape into a ball shape. Then use extra tape to wrap around the ball, sticky side out. Have some extra masking tape pieces available to reapply during the activity as needed. Also draw a large bull's-eye target on a sheet of newsprint.

You'll want the distance from the target to be short enough so students occasionally hit the target, but long enough so they can't consistently hit the target. Depending on the size of your target bull's-eye and the masking tape ball, you may need to experiment with the spacing.

The Point ➤

Here are some suggestions for helping the dramas run smoothly: Have groups choose a good reader to act as the narrator. As the narrator reads his or her verses from the Bible, the actors can act out their parts, also speaking their lines. If you have smaller groups, some kids could play more than one role.

You could provide some optional props for the dramas, such as cloth scraps or towels to be used for quick costumes.

Have students line up about six to ten feet behind the target. **Say: You'll each have three chances to throw this ball at the target. Try to hit the bull's-eye on the target all three times. If you hit the target, you'll get more chances.**

Give each preteen three chances. If a student does hit the target, give him or her extra throws until he or she misses. After everyone has had a turn,

ask:

• **How hard was it to hit the target? Explain.**

• **How many times do you think you could hit the target before you would miss?**

Say: Eventually, we all would miss the target. In fact, this is the meaning of the word *sin*. **We miss the target of pleasing God all the time with our lives. But that's where God's grace comes in. Today we're going to see how ➤We can live for God because of Jesus' forgiveness. Let's see how.**

Bible Connection

What Is Grace? *(up to 10 minutes)*

Give each preteen a photocopy of the "God's Grace for Me" handout (p. 39) and a pen. Have students form pairs or trios, and give each group a Bible. **Say: Read the listed Scriptures from your handout, and then write your summary of grace. You can work with your partners, but I want each of you to write a personal summary. I'll circulate around the room to assist you if you need it.**

Allow pairs or trios about five minutes to complete their summaries.

Ask:

• **What did you learn about grace from this activity?**

Say: Grace is what God gives us. ➤We can live for God because of Jesus' forgiveness. Let's look at examples of God's forgiveness.

Forgiveness Stories *(up to 20 minutes)*

Have your students form two groups. Assign the story of the prodigal (lost) son in Luke 15:11-32 to the first group. To the other group, assign the story of Peter's denial of Jesus in Luke 22:52-62 and Peter's reinstatement by Jesus in John 21:15-19. **Say: In your groups, read the passages for your story, and then plan how to act out your story with your group members. After you've prepared your drama, you'll perform it for the class.**

Give groups about five to eight minutes to prepare their dramas. Circulate during this time and offer assistance as needed.

When groups are ready, have groups perform their dramas. Lead the applause after each group's presentation. Then have preteens discuss the following questions in their groups:

Ask:

• **How was forgiveness shown in these stories?**

• **How would you have felt if you had been either the lost son or Peter before forgiveness was given?**

• **What is it like when you need forgiveness for something you've done wrong?**

Allow a few minutes for groups to discuss the questions. Then **say: The lost son and Peter both found themselves in difficult situations. Only God's grace could help them, and the same is true for us. ➤We can live for God because of Jesus' forgiveness. Let's look at how God's grace applies to our lives.**

◄ *The Point*

Life Application

Forgiveness Thanks *(up to 10 minutes)*

Give each preteen a Bible, a "Forgiveness Letter" handout (p. 40), and a pen. Allow students to spread out and work individually on their handouts.

When kids have finished with their handouts, ask a volunteer to read aloud Philippians 3:12-14.

Say: The Apostle Paul wrote these words to explain how he lived his Christian life. Paul wasn't perfect and neither are we. But we can follow his example of forgetting what's behind—sin forgiven by God—and pressing on toward the goal.

Ask:

• **How does knowing you're forgiven motivate you to live more fully for God?**

Have preteens form pairs. **Say: Take turns telling your partner one way you'll live for God this week.**

Allow preteens a minute to do this before moving to the study's closing.

Forgiveness Banquet *(up to 10 minutes)*

Say: The father celebrated his lost son's return by having a banquet. Let's celebrate our forgiveness with food and music!

Set out snacks and drinks for students to enjoy. Play praise or worship CDs in the background as you enjoy the refreshments. You may want to sing some of the praise songs as a closing prayer.

Wrap-Up Option 2

Clean Slate *(up to 10 minutes)*

Have preteens line up next to one another, facing you. You may have more than one line if you have a large group. While students line up, quickly write several words (the words are not important) on a piece of paper. Hold up the piece of paper for students to see. **Say: The words written on this piece of paper represent the times you've fallen short of living for God in any area of your life. Think about a time you've fallen short.**

Ask students to each turn around in a full circle and face the same spot again. As they turn, flip the paper to reveal the blank side. **Say: Just as the words on this paper were replaced by a blank sheet, your forgiven sins give you a "clean slate" to live for God. Now go live for him!**

Close your study with a prayer, pausing to allow students to silently thank God for his forgiveness and guidance in their lives.

Extra-Time Tips

Modern Prodigal—Have your kids rewrite the parable of the prodigal son as a modern situation. You may want to put the parable in a church newsletter, or have kids act it out for the whole congregation.

My Forgiveness Story—Before the study, ask adult or teen volunteers to share stories of God's forgiveness in their lives.

God's Grace for Me

Look up the following Scriptures: John 1:16-18; Ephesians 2:8-9; Hebrews 4:14-16; and 1 John 2:1-2.
Then write a summary in your own words of what grace means for you.

Read Philippians 3:12-14. Think about this question: What does God want me to do after he grants me forgiveness for something I've done wrong?

Think about a situation in your life in which you need or have needed God's forgiveness. Write a letter to God describing the situation and thanking God for forgiving you. Then write what you think you've learned from the experience and how you can apply the principles of Philippians 3:12-14 to live for God more fully in the future.

Forgiveness Letter

his study series has helped preteens see who they are and what purpose God has for them. Here's an idea that can help build on what preteens have learned about living fully for God.

Have a caring and serving day. Plan a Saturday of helping projects that preteens can do for church members or people in your community. Encourage students to serve in ways that match their gifts and abilities.Have students announce the event and explain that they will call or e-mail church members to sign up people for the event. Enlist volunteers to drive and supervise groups of preteens at each caring site. Preteens should be able to handle some of the following tasks: cleaning houses or cars, raking leaves or general yardwork, and some painting projects.

Have preteens report results to the church on the Sunday following the service day. Plan a celebration lunch after your worship service to allow preteens to talk about the experience.

Faith 4 Life: Why God Made Me

Please help Group Publishing, Inc., continue to provide innovative and useful resources for ministry. Please take a moment to fill out this evaluation and mail or fax it to us. Thanks!

Group Publishing, Inc.
Attention: Product Development
P.O. Box 481
Loveland, CO 80539
Fax: (970) 292-4370

● ● ●

1. As a whole, this book has been (circle one)
   not very helpful   very helpful
   1   2   3   4   5   6   7   8   9   10

2. The best things about this book:

3. Ways this book could be improved:

4. Things I will change because of this book:

5. Other books I'd like to see Group publish in the future:

6. Would you be interested in field-testing future Group products and giving us your feedback? If so, please fill in the information below:

Name ____

Church Name ____

Denomination _______________________ Church Size___________________________

Church Address ____

City_______________________ State ______________ ZIP ______________

Church Phone ____

E-mail ____

Look for the Whole Family of Faith 4 Life Bible Studies!

Preteen Books

Being Responsible
Getting Along With Others
God in My Life
Going Through Tough Times

How to Make Great Choices
Peer Pressure
The Bible and Me
Why God Made Me

Junior High Books

Becoming a Christian
Fighting Temptation
Finding Your Identity
Friends

God's Purpose for Me
My Life as a Christian
Understanding the Bible
Who Is God?

Senior High Books

Applying God's Word
Believing in Jesus
Family Matters
Is There Life After High School?

Prayer
Sexuality
Sharing Your Faith
Your Christian ID

Coming Soon...

For Preteens

Building Friendships
Handling Conflict

Succeeding in School
What's a Christian?

For Junior High

Choosing Wisely
How to Pray

My Family Life
Sharing Jesus

For Senior High

Christian Character
Following Jesus

Worshipping 24/7
Your Relationships

More Preteen Ministry Resources!

The Preteen Worker's Encyclopedia of Bible-Teaching Ideas

Make the New Testament come alive to your preteens and help them discover Bible truths in a big way! In this comprehensive collection, you get nearly 200 creative ideas and activities including: object lessons, skits, games, devotions, service projects, creative prayers, affirmations, creative readings, retreats, parties, trips and travel, and music ideas.

Flexible for any group setting, you'll easily find the perfect idea with helpful Scripture and theme indexes.

ISBN 0-7644-2425-4

Dynamic Preteen Ministry

Gordon West & Becki West

Maximize ministry to preteens as they make the difficult transition from childhood to adolescence. Both children's and youth workers will better understand the minds and emotions of 10- to 14-year-olds, "bridge the gap" between children's ministry and youth ministry.

ISBN 0-7644-2084-4

The Ultimate Book of Preteen Devotions

Take the challenge of ministering to preteens to the edge! They're sure to connect with these 75 Bible-based devotions. From setting goals, to materialism, to dealing with divorce—these topics and many others are included in the 6 big themes found in this ultimate book:

- Faith
- Friends
- Family
- School
- My World
- Special Days

Plus, easy-prep devotional activities use different learning styles—and multiple intelligences—to reach all preteens. Scripture index included.

ISBN 0-7644-2588-9

Connect with Preteens In Dynamic Ways!

No-Miss Lessons for Preteen Kids

Here are 22 faith-building lessons that keep 5th- and 6th-graders coming back! Children's workers get active-learning lessons dealing with faith…self-esteem…relationships…choices…and age-appropriate service projects that any preteen class can do!

ISBN 0-7644-2015-1

No-Miss Lessons for Preteen Kids 2

Enjoy ministering to your preteens like never before! This flexible resource features 20 action-packed, easy-to-teach lessons that talk about the stuff of life in the preteen world. Stuff like the Internet and media, how to get along with family and friends, faith foundations based on God and Jesus, and many others! These lessons and the 13 bonus, "can't-miss" service project ideas will challenge kids, grow their faith, and give them practical ideas for living out their deepening faith in meaningful ways!

ISBN 0-7644-2290-1

The Ultimate Book of Preteen Games

They're not children. Not teenagers. What do you do with preteens? Have a blast! Start with these 100 games they'll love! In the process, you'll break down cliques, build relationships, explore relevant Bible truths, give thought-provoking challenges, and have high-energy fun!

ISBN 0-7644-2291-X